THIS BOOK IS LOVINGLY DEDICATED TO
THE MEMORY OF RITA'S FATHER, JAY WINKLER

My Art My World

Rita Winkler

WITH HELEN WINKLER AND MARK WINKLER

Second Story Press

I'm RITA.

And I love making art.
This is a painting I made of myself!
Do you think it looks like me?

I draw whenever I can —
In the morning when the sun comes out,
and then when I see
the moon before bed.

I take this bus to my job at a coffee shop.

And this is the cash register where I put the money from the people who buy brownies, cookies, drinks, and chocolate bars from me.

Learning to use this machine was hard but now I am great at it.

I never give the wrong change. Well, almost never.

Can you believe that someone at the coffee shop was carrying fish in a bag once? They were so cute.

I think they came from a lake. Maybe the same one where I swim every summer.

Do you think the fish ever saw me in the water there?

I didn't recognize them, but maybe they remembered me. That would be very funny.

It annoys me that pesky telemarketers interrupt me when I'm busy.

we are not
home Leve
us Olaone
Thank Yoy

Rita

Now I leave this drawing with a message beside the phone.

I hope there are no more calls!

I love to visit my Uncle Mark who lives in
New York City.

There are so many people going in every
direction. The buildings are huge.

And cars honk and honk and honk some more.
I sometimes need to cover my ears.

New York feels like this wild piece of cut paper
that I made.

My art teacher says it reminds her of the taxis
and streets there.

My art is different every season.

In the spring, the trees seem to get bigger when the leaves and the colors come back.

Summer flowers make me feel happy.

They look like they are smiling at everyone.

Fall brings big, round pumpkins that my friends sometimes carve into faces.

And poppies. The poppies I paint are for remembering our soldiers.

They make gray days a little brighter for me.

Winter is sometimes too cold.
But as I look through my window I think
it can be very beautiful.

It's also a great holiday time. I can't wait to see the wonderful fireworks on New Year's Eve.

Just like the different seasons, I love that people don't all look the same.

Every person is special, so each face I draw is special too.

Here are my friends Carolyn and Sammy.

Sometimes
I draw
people
who I see
in my
imagination.

This one
I call the
*Lady With
the Purple
Arms*.

Do you think this snowman face
looks like anyone you know?

My mom says it's important
that I have other hobbies.

So every day I choose one
of my favorites.

Here I am in dance class.

Recognize me
in the middle?

I learned to do sign language for the times
I meet a new friend who is deaf.

I was even in a choir once where we signed
the words of the songs.

It made me feel very proud.

I still practice so I don't forget.

YOGA
clams me
down

And yoga is very much fun too.

My teacher says I'm excellent at stretching
and bending.

The different yoga positions have names
that will make you laugh:

Twisted chair, dragon, elephant, and even
happy baby.

Here is me doing downward dog.

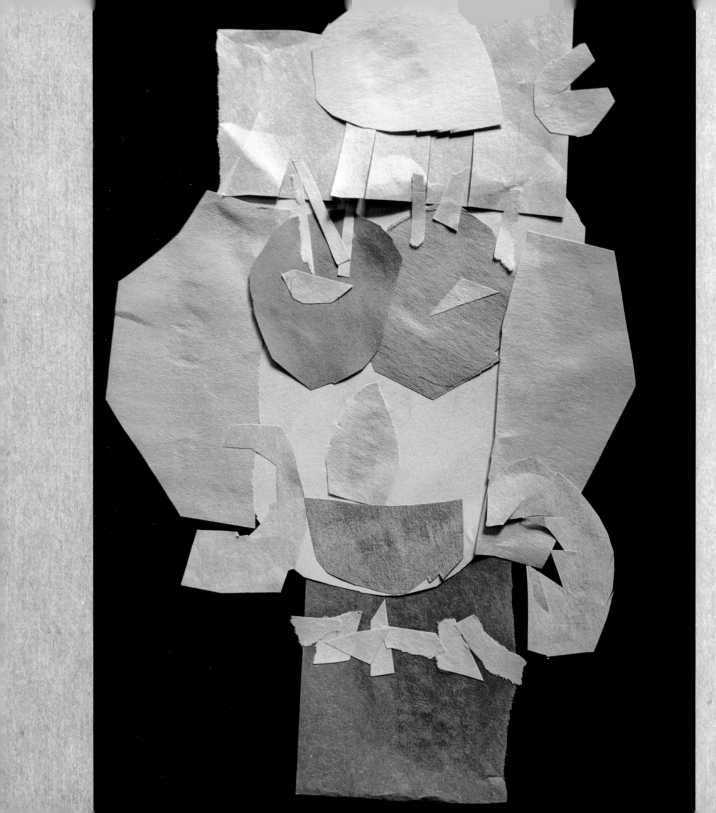

I'm lucky that my days are so much fun.
Yoga, dancing, sign language, the coffee shop,
my wacky Uncle Mark, my wonderful mom,
even the pesky telemarketers.

But most of all, I love making my art.

So now you've seen my art. And my world.
Thanks for letting me show them to you.

And just in case you forgot,

I'm RITA.

About Rita

Rita and other people born with Down syndrome look a little different. They may have medical problems and need help with learning. Each person with Down syndrome is unique and, like everyone, needs the opportunity to learn and to live a satisfying life. Rita graduated high school, has a job, enjoys drama, reading, spending time with her friends, and being active on social media. Born in Calgary, Rita has two sisters, and now lives with her mother in Toronto.

To learn more about Down syndrome, visit the Canadian Down Syndrome Society website: **cdss.ca**

And about the Dani Day program where Rita continues to learn and have fun: **dani-toronto.com**

Common Ground is where Rita works: **commongroundco-op.ca**

Thank you to Bob Cortez who provided the encouragement and feedback when this book was just an idea. We would also like to thank Rita's art teachers Anna Gruzman (Dani-Toronto) and Karina Viovy (L'Arche London) who guided Rita in her creative growth. And to Ferg Devins, James Sauli, Harold Slazer, and Rita's sisters, Rachel and Leora, who helped in so many ways to make this book a reality. Finally, we would like to thank the staff at Second Story Press for the talent and care they invested in this book. In particular, Melissa Kaita for her outstanding graphics and reproductions of Rita's artwork, and Margie Wolfe, who took a leap of faith and believed there was a story to be told.

———————

Library and Archives Canada Cataloguing in Publication

Title: My art, my world / Rita Winkler.
Names: Winkler, Rita, 1987- author, artist.
Identifiers: Canadiana 20210136022 | ISBN 9781772602142 (hardcover)
Subjects: LCSH: Winkler, Rita, 1987-—Juvenile literature. | LCSH: Down syndrome patients as artists—Ontario—Toronto—Juvenile literature. | LCSH: Painting, Canadian—Ontario—Toronto—21st century—Juvenile literature.
Classification: LCC HD249.W56 A4 2021 | DDC j759.11—dc23

Inspired by Helen Winkler and Mark Winkler

Edited by Margie Wolfe

Photo on page 24 by Leon Balaban

Printed and bound in China

Second Story Press gratefully acknowledges the support of the Ontario Arts Council and the Canada Council for the Arts for our publishing program. We acknowledge the financial support of the Government of Canada through the Canada Book Fund.

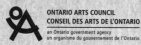
ONTARIO ARTS COUNCIL
CONSEIL DES ARTS DE L'ONTARIO
an Ontario government agency
un organisme du gouvernement de l'Ontario

Canada Council   Conseil des Arts
for the Arts   du Canada

Funded by the   Financé par le
Government of   gouvernement
Canada   du Canada    Canada

Published by
Second Story Press
20 Maud Street, Suite 401
Toronto, Ontario, Canada
M5V 2M5
www.secondstorypress.ca